Feathered Dinosaurs
OF China

Gregory Wenzel

ini Charlesbridge

For my mom, who let me keep lizards
and caimans in my bedroom and
encouraged me to pursue a life in
natural history—G. W.

Special thanks to Dr. Peter Dodson,
Professor of Anatomy and Professor of
Earth and Environmental Science,
University of Pennsylvania

Published by Charlesbridge
85 Main Street
Watertown, MA 02472
(617) 926-0329
www.charlesbridge.com

Library of Congress Cataloging-in-Publication Data
Wenzel, Gregory C.
Feathered dinosaurs of China / written and illustrated by Gregory
Wenzel.
  p. cm.
  Summary: Discusses the feathered dinosaurs of prehistoric China
and their relationship to modern birds. Includes index.
  ISBN 1-57091-561-X (reinforced for library use)
  ISBN 1-57091-562-8 (softcover)
1. Dinosaurs—China—Juvenile literature. 2. Birds, Fossil—Juvenile
literature. 3. Birds—Origin—Juvenile literature. [1. Dinosaurs.
2. Birds. 3. Birds, Fossil. 4. Paleontology—China.] I. Title.
QE861.9.C6 W46 2003
567.9—dc21   2002010493

Printed in Korea
(hc) 10 9 8 7 6 5 4 3 2 1   (sc) 10 9 8 7 6 5 4 3 2 1

Illustrations done in acrylics on paper
Text type set in Adobe Goudy and display type set in Amigo
Color separated, printed, and bound by Sung In Printing,
  South Korea
Production supervision by Linda Jackson
Designed by Susan Mallory Sherman

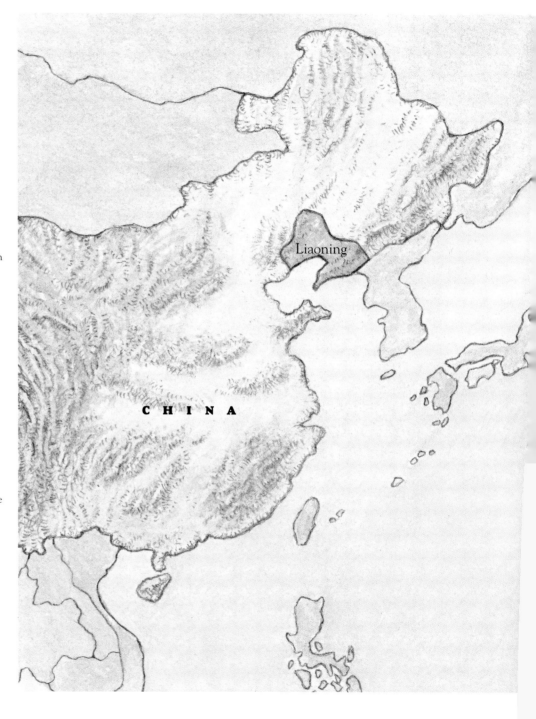

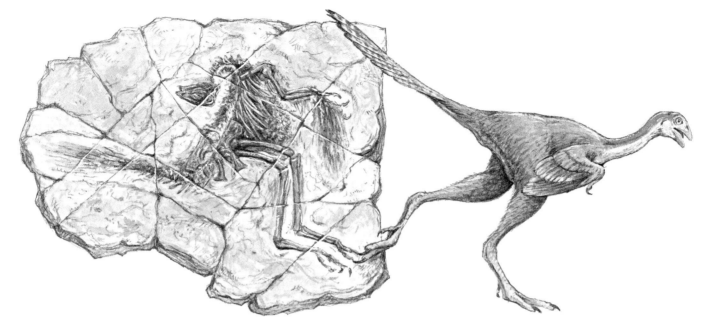

 Some of the best fossils ever found are being discovered in ancient lakebeds in China. Not just an animal here and a plant there—these fossils show a whole ecosystem including feathered dinosaurs. Scientists are getting a rare look at a prehistoric world.

Unusually fine details are preserved in these fossils from Liaoning Province. They show the delicate wings of insects, veins of leaves, fragile skin, feathers, and soft anatomy, such as internal organs. Many animals are fossilized as complete skeletons, with all of the bones in their proper positions.

These clues tell us about the dinosaurs that roamed prehistoric China. Paleontologists know that one type of dinosaur liked to eat tiny mammals and lizards. How could they tell? The mammals' bones were fossilized in the dinosaur's stomach. Unlaid eggs are visible in the fossil of another dinosaur. There are even examples of color patterns on the fossils of insect wings and dinosaur tail feathers.

The layers, or strata, in the earth's crust where we find these remains are called the Yixian Formation. They date from the Early Cretaceous Period, 124 million years ago. Millions of fossils have been excavated from the Yixian sites. So far, hundreds of different fish and invertebrates that lived in the lakes have been found, some preserved as entire schools of fish or beds of clams. Beautifully preserved remains of reptiles, dinosaurs, mammals, and birds record what life was like around the margins of the lake. Plant and insect fossils fill out the picture of the environment where these fascinating creatures made their home.

Based on the fossil evidence, we can recreate the prehistoric ecosystem of the Liaoning lakes.

Let's step back 124 million years. The scene looks nothing like present-day northeastern China. It is a vast, flat landscape dotted with shallow lakes and ponds. Covering the land are forests filled with dense vegetation and exotic trees. A diverse community of creatures both familiar and strange thrives in this warm, green environment. We'll spend a day meeting some of the inhabitants, including the extraordinary feathered dinosaurs.

The morning sun climbs above the treetops, bright light shimmering on the lake. Dragonflies zoom low over the water as they hunt for insects. Fallen trees lie half-submerged along the shoreline, their bleached trunks lined with basking turtles.

There are lily pads on the surface of the water, and a tangle of reeds and horsetails growing along the waterline. In the damp shadows, salamanders hunt for tiny arthropods. A *Callobatrachus*, a small frog, watches a dragonfly. A flick of a sticky tongue, and the insect is breakfast for the amphibian.

Tree ferns, cycads, and cypress border the lake, where the constant hum of insects is occasionally broken by the loud call of a bird. Another very warm day is beginning.

Nearby, twigs snap and feet rustle the dry leaves. Something big is moving.

. . .flick of a sticky tongue. . .

A herd of *Jinzhousaurus* is foraging for food in the forest underbrush. These are some of the largest of the Liaoning dinosaurs, up to 20 feet (6 meters) long. As they feed, their heads swing from side to side, snipping off plants with their horny beaks. The sharp edges of the beaks shear plants like scissors. Flat, grinding teeth chew the leafy matter before it's swallowed. The *Jinzhousaurus* are related to the *Iguanodon*, which lives in Europe during this time period.

Usually on all fours, they rear up on their hind legs to reach foliage on high branches. After plucking off mouthfuls, the dinosaurs drop back down to eat. Like many large herbivores, the *Jinzhousaurus* spend most of their time eating. They could eat all of the plants in one spot in minutes, so the herd keeps moving. Their shuffling feet kick up the litter on the forest floor, flushing insects and small animals into the open.

. . .sharp edges of the beaks shear plants. . .

A *Jinzhousaurus* steps on a rotted log. The furry mammal hiding underneath barely avoids being crushed and scurries to find new shelter. This is an *Eomaia*, no bigger than a mouse. Its sharp, pointed teeth show that it feeds primarily on insects. Mammals of this time are tiny, nocturnal creatures. In a world dominated by agile hunting dinosaurs, it's safer to hide during the day.

As the huge *Jinzhousaurus* browse, many small creatures are scared from their hiding places. Beetles and other insects fly up with every footfall, and lizards rush for cover.

A *Sinornithosaurus* hunts for prey disturbed by the herbivores. The feathery predator is alert to the slightest movement.

...alert to the slightest movement...

11

The *Sinornithosaurus* belongs to the dromaeosaur family of hunting dinosaurs. The inside toe of each foot has a large curved claw, poised to catch and hold prey. Folded against the body, its arms are covered in long feathers and look like wings. Just visible beneath this plumage are three long fingers with sharp claws. Hair-like feathers cover the rest of this five-foot-long (1.5 meters) theropod, a meat-eating dinosaur.

The *Eomaia* is sent scrambling again, and the eagle-sized predator is after it. In a flurry of leaves and twigs, the *Sinornithosaurus* stops, nearly crashing into a fallen tree.

The *Eomaia* is held firmly by a big foot claw. Sharp, recurved, serrated teeth lining the hunter's beak make short work of the meal. The hunter moves onto the lakeshore.

. . .predator is after it. . .

...flock of birds glides in...

Near the water, two pterosaurs squabble over a dead fish. The *Sinornithosaurus* startles one of them, an *Eosipterus*, into flight.

The *Eosipterus* is the bigger of the two flying reptiles, with a wingspan of four feet (1.25 meters). Its wing is an expanse of skin stretching from the side of its body, attached to the edge of a single long finger. Tiny stiff rods in the skin, called aktinofibrils, keep the wing rigid during flight. Short, thick fur covers the rest of the body to insulate this warm-blooded flier.

The smaller pterosaur, a *Dendrorhynchoides*, snatches the prize with needle-like teeth and quickly flies away.

A large flock of birds glides in to perch in the trees along the shore. These are *Confuciusornis*, the most common Liaoning birds. Unlike modern birds, they have three-fingered hands with sharp claws on the inside of their short wings. They look like the hands of theropod dinosaurs. The males have two very long, ribbon-like tail feathers, most likely used for display and to attract females.

On the ground below, something moves in and out of the shadows.

A *Caudipteryx*, a small theropod, heads to the shore for a drink. It stops to peck at small rounded pebbles scattered in a dry streambed. The *Caudipteryx* has no grinding teeth, just a row of forward-pointing teeth at the front of its upper jaw. It swallows these little stones to help mash food in its gizzard, a part of its stomach.

The *Caudipteryx* passes by several *Manchurosuchus* sprawled on the sand. When it gets too close, one of the crocodylians lunges.

The theropod leaps into the air, spreads its striped tail feathers, and opens its arms wide. Together, the arm and tail feathers make an effective threat display. With a squawk, the *Caudipteryx* lands safely out of the crocodylian's reach.

Turtles, startled by the commotion, drop into the water.

. . .stops to peck at small rounded pebbles. . .

16

On the lake bottom, a softshell turtle, a *Manchurochelys*, buries itself in muck. Tadpoles wriggle past a colony of clams.

The lake bottom is alive with small creatures. Snails graze on algae on submerged leaves. A dragonfly nymph lies in wait to ambush its tiny prey: aquatic insects, worms, small crustaceans, even small fish. Huge mayfly larvae, nearly three inches (7.5 centimeters) long, wave leaf-like gills along their sides.

Many fish species live in these warm waters. Some lurk in the shadows under lily pads, hunting smaller fish. Others, such as the *Protosephurus*, detect small prey by probing the sediment with their snouts.

A school of tiny *Lycoptera* is gliding through the water, but suddenly darts away. A *Hyphalosaurus*, a lizard-like aquatic predator, is coming. Its long neck arcs from side to side as it searches for small fish and insects.

. . .long neck arcs from side to side. . .

Back on shore, Liaoning creatures seek shelter from the midday heat. The high-pitched drone of cicadas fills the air.

In the shade of tree ferns, a pair of *Beipiaosaurus* stays cool by panting. Like all feathered creatures, they're warm-blooded and can overheat when it's hot.

At seven feet (2 meters) long, the *Beipiaosaurus* are some of the largest feathered dinosaurs known. Feathers, many more than one foot (30.5 centimeters) long, cover their bodies down to their feet. Their arms are fully feathered as well, and their hands tipped with recurved claws. Although these claws look fearsome, the *Beipiaosaurus* feed on plants. Maybe the claws were used for defense, or to help dig for food.

. . .high-pitched drone of cicadas. . .

On the lakefront, a four-foot-long (1.2 meters) *Sinosauropteryx* swishes its long tail as it searches for an afternoon meal. With 64 vertebrae, its tail is proportionately the longest of any known theropod. Its small arms, tucked against its body when it runs, are not covered with broad feathers like the *Sinornithosaurus* and *Caudipteryx*. The arms have the same hair-like plumage that covers the rest of its body.

A lizard suns itself on a piece of driftwood, eyeing a striped moth nearby. The *Sinosauropteryx* spies the potential meal and dashes forward. Before the lizard can react, a clawed, three-toed foot pins it in place until sharp teeth snap it up.

The lizard's tail still dangling from its mouth, the *Sinosauropteryx* freezes and cocks its head. There's activity in the distance. It swallows the scaly snack headfirst and moves off to investigate.

. . .sharp teeth snap it up. . .

23

Near the water the *Sinosauropteryx* finds a family group of *Microraptor* scavenging the carcass of a *Psittacosaurus*, a type of horned dinosaur. The *Microraptor* is truly tiny, the smallest adult dinosaur known. Just 16 inches (41 centimeters) long, it could rest in a human hand. It's a dromaeosaur and, like most hunters, will take advantage of a free meal.

The *Microraptor* flock protests noisily, but they're no match for the *Sinosauropteryx*. They pester the intruder while it feeds. The *Sinosauropteryx* eats its fill and moves on.

The *Microraptor* family moves back to feed and is joined by several birds that snatch small pieces off the carcass. These are *Protopteryx*. Like the *Confuciusornis*, they have three-fingered hands with sharp claws. As they squabble over the carcass, it's hard to tell dromaeosaur from bird.

. . .they squabble over the carcass. . .

25

. . .another gives chase. . .

One *Protopteryx*, with a small piece of meat in its beak, takes off toward the trees. Another gives chase. The two birds fight for the meat in midair. As they quarrel, the morsel is dropped.

A *Protarchaeopteryx*, a smaller relative of the *Caudipteryx*, has been watching the fight. It snatches the scrap as soon as it hits the ground and speeds away from the pursuing birds.

The small dinosaur eludes the *Protopteryx* by running into the herd of *Jinzhousaurus*. They take little notice of the theropod. The *Protarchaeopteryx* runs off with the scrap in its beak to give to hatchlings in a nearby nest.

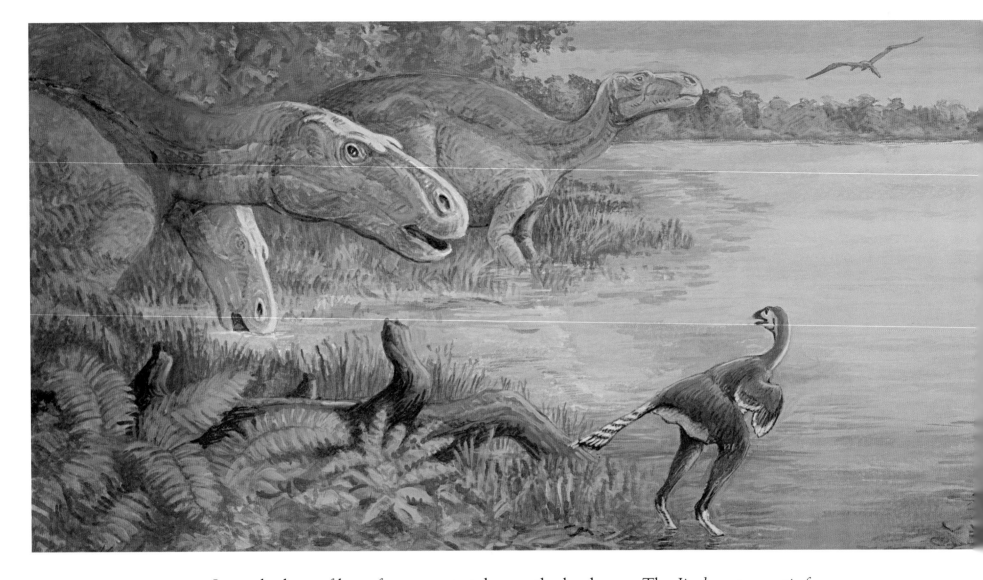

Long shadows of late afternoon stretch over the landscape. The *Jinzhousaurus* stir from their heat-induced rest. Many head toward the lake to drink. Pterosaurs wheel lazily on the warm air, while birds of all kinds flit from tree to tree. The *Microraptor* flock, full from their meal, rests in a thicket, as a pair of *Sinornithosaurus* picks over the *Psittacosaurus* carcass.

At the water's edge, the *Caudipteryx* is interrupted mid-bath by the thirsty *Jinzhousaurus*.

It tries to scare them with its feather display, but the towering plant-eaters are not impressed and the *Caudipteryx* is forced to retreat.

Down the shoreline, the *Sinosauropteryx* is hunting again. It may get lucky and catch a night creature that came out too early. In the fading light, a chorus of frogs begins to croak. As the day ends, we leave Liaoning.

 During the time of feathered dinosaurs, volcanoes would periodically shower ash and poisonous gases on the lakeside communities. Animals would die and sink to the bottom of the lakes, where they were quickly covered in an accumulating sediment of volcanic ash.

Rapid burial prevented decay. It allowed the soft anatomy to remain intact, and the fine-grain of the ash preserved structures in minute detail. These special conditions are the reason for the high quality of the Yixian fossils.

Not all of the plants and animals were killed in these eruptions. The survivors would gradually reclaim the environment and thrive—until the next volcanic event. Over long periods of time this process repeated itself, building up layer after layer of entombed organisms.

For millions of years, the fossils remained hidden in the earth's crust. Eventually, the sedimentary layers were pushed up by geologic forces and uncovered by erosion. Today, paleontologists find beautifully preserved feathered dinosaurs in these ancient lakebeds.

These feathered remains help us to understand more about dinosaurs. Plumage on Liaoning's theropods suggests that feathers were a common feature in many types of related dinosaurs.

We know that dinosaurs were warm-blooded since they were wrapped in nature's most efficient insulating device, feathers. Only animals that produce their own heat and maintain a constant temperature need to be insulated.

Birds and dinosaurs share over 100 similarities in their bodies, including hollow bones; clawed, three-toed feet; unique ankle and wrist joints; and feathers. Based on the evidence, we can say that birds are not only the living descendants of dinosaurs—birds *are* dinosaurs. We can think of all modern birds as living, breathing, feathered dinosaurs.

Glossary / Index

Author's Note

Dinosaur discoveries are still happening today. I've been lucky enough to be a part of dinosaur excavations in the United States, as a staff member for the Judith River Dinosaur Institute, an organization specializing in the excavation, preparation, and study of Cretaceous dinosaurs in Montana. Recently, that group excavated a juvenile *Brachylophosaurus* specimen, one of the most complete dinosaur fossils ever found.

Creating illustrations of dinosaurs takes imagination as well as scientific knowledge. Looking at bones and fossils is just the first step. Interpreting the evidence, based on an understanding of animal anatomy, provides the information I need to picture dinosaurs as living animals.

A note on pronunciation: Scientific names of plants and animals are made by combining two or more Latin, Greek, or other root words. Pronouncing these names isn't always easy, and many dinosaur experts disagree on the "right" way to do it. The pronunciations listed here keep the root words separate and distinct, to help you find similarities among the names.